ROBERT D. VANDALL

PRELUDES

Complete with CD

24 Original Piano Solos

in All Major and Minor Keys

(UK Exam Grades 2–7)

Cover design: Tom Gerou
Music engraving: Linda Lusk

Alfred

Copyright © MMVI by Alfred Publishing Co., Inc.
All rights reserved.   Printed in USA.
ISBN 0-7390-4317-X

Volume 1

	Page	Track
Prelude No. 1 in C Major	2	1
Prelude No. 2 in D Major	4	2
Prelude No. 3 in E Minor	6	3
Prelude No. 4 in F Major	8	4
Prelude No. 5 in G Major	10	5
Prelude No. 6 in A Major	12	6
Prelude No. 7 in B Minor	14	7

Volume 2

Prelude No. 8 in C♯ Minor	16	8
Prelude No. 9 in D Minor	18	9
Prelude No. 10 in E♭ Major	20	10
Prelude No. 11 in F Minor	22	11
Prelude No. 12 in G Minor	25	12
Prelude No. 13 in A♭ Major	28	13
Prelude No. 14 in B Major	30	14

Additional Preludes for Second Edition

Prelude No. 22 in E♭ Minor	33	15
Prelude No. 23 in F♯ Minor	34	16
Prelude No. 24 in B♭ Minor	36	17

Volume 3

Prelude No. 15 in C Minor	39	18
Prelude No. 16 in D♭ Major	42	19
Prelude No. 17 in E Major	45	20
Prelude No. 18 in F♯ Major	48	21
Prelude No. 19 in G♯ Minor	52	22
Prelude No. 20 in A Minor	54	23
Prelude No. 21 in B♭ Major	57	24

Prelude No. 1 in C Major

Robert D. Vandall

no pedal

Prelude No. 2 in D Major

Robert D. Vandall

Prelude No. 3 in E Minor

Robert D. Vandall

Prelude No. 4 in F Major

Robert D. Vandall

Prelude No. 5 in G Major

Robert D. Vandall

Prelude No. 6 in A Major

Robert D. Vandall

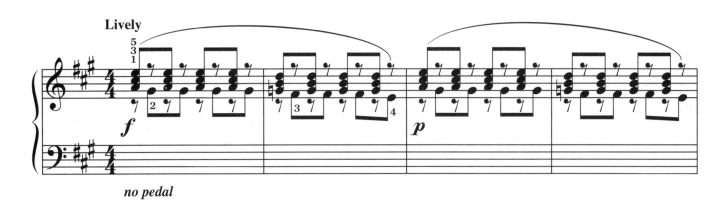

no pedal

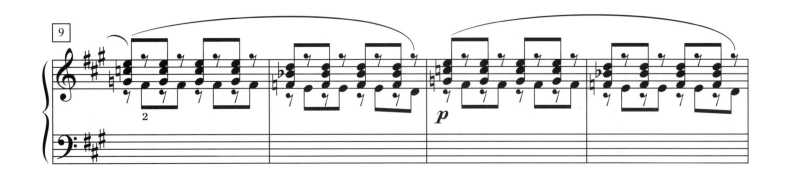

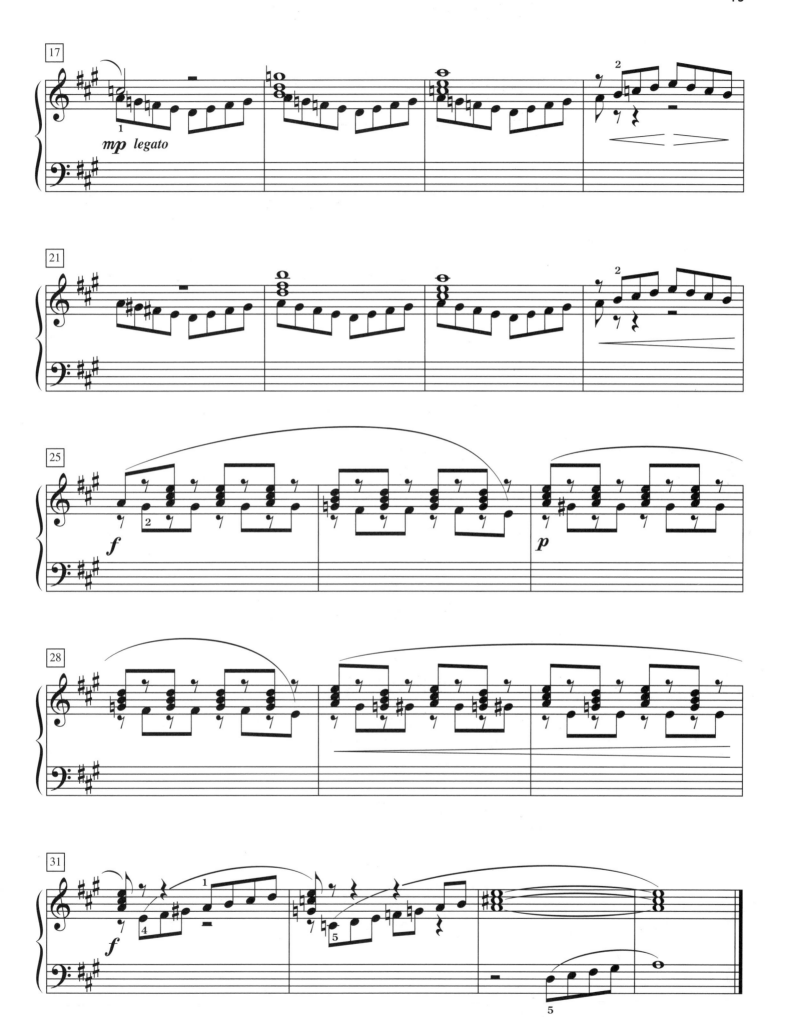

Prelude No. 7 in B Minor
Chaconne

Robert D. Vandall

Prelude No. 8 in C# Minor

Robert D. Vandall

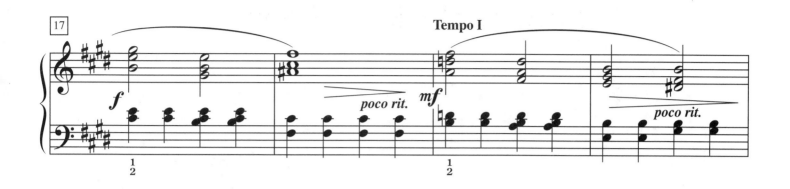

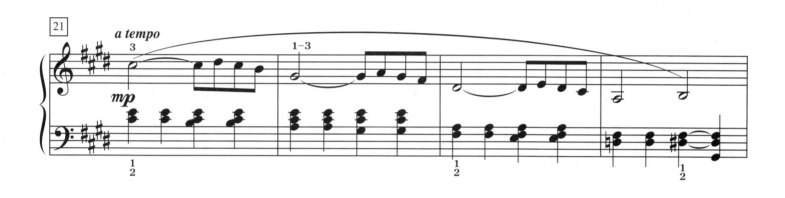

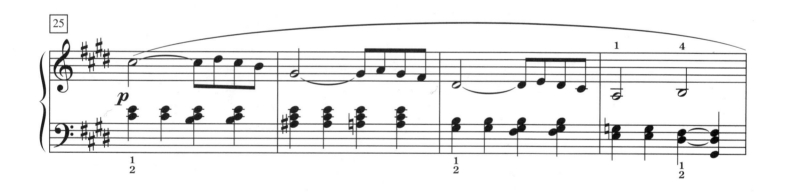

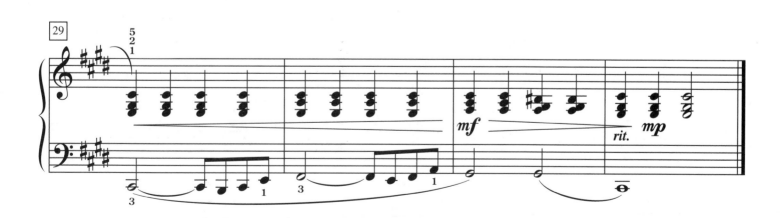

Prelude No. 9 in D Minor

Robert D. Vandall

Prelude No. 10 in E♭ Major

Robert D. Vandall

Prelude No. II in F Minor

Robert D. Vandall

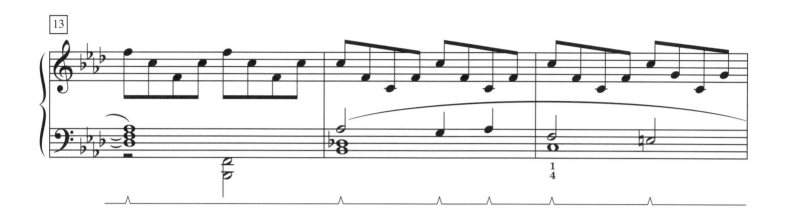

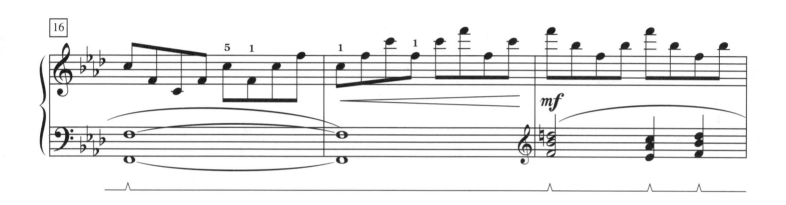

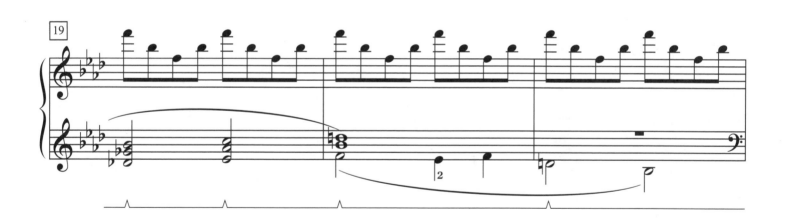

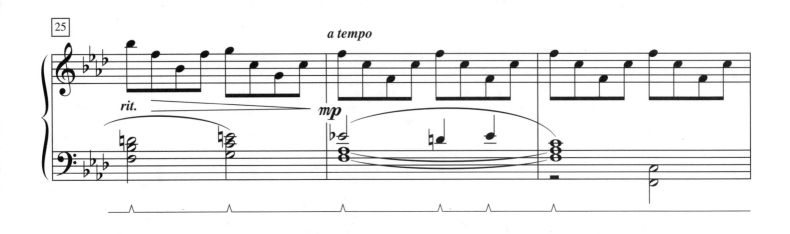

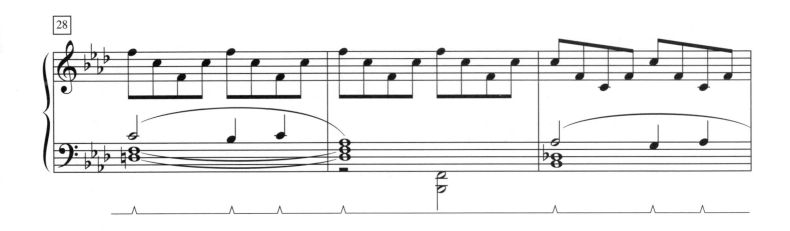

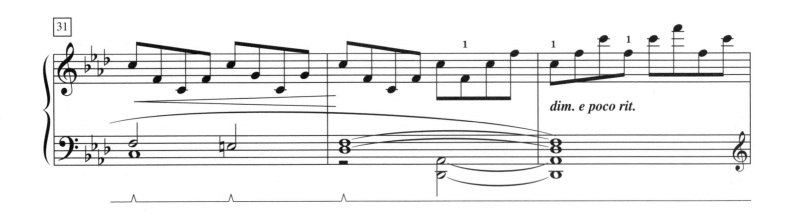

Prelude No. 12 in G Minor

Robert D. Vandall

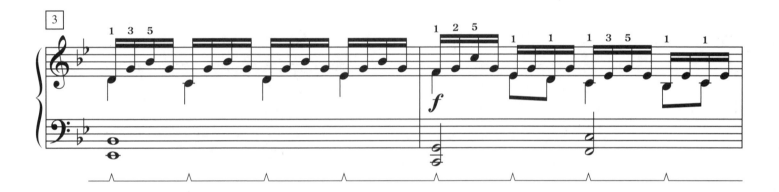

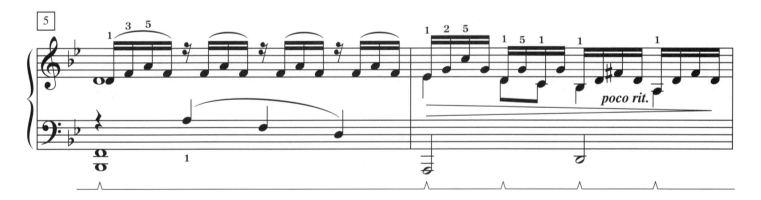

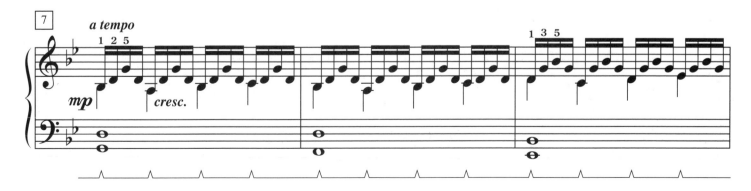

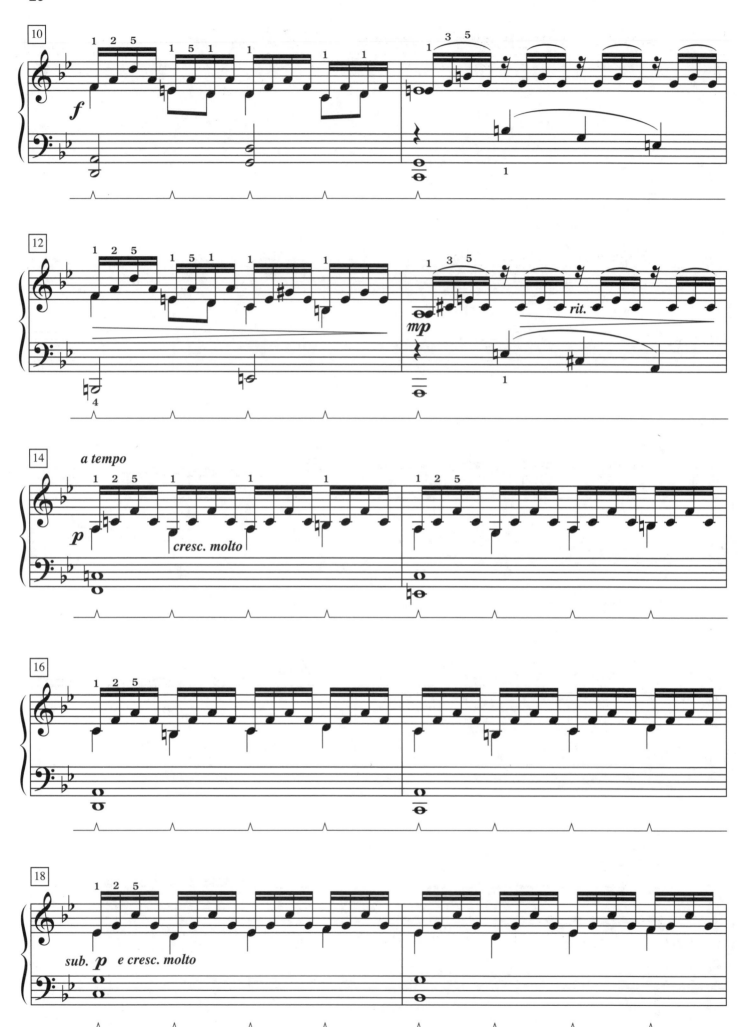

Prelude No. 13 in A♭ Major

Robert D. Vandall

Prelude No. 14 in B Major

Robert D. Vandall

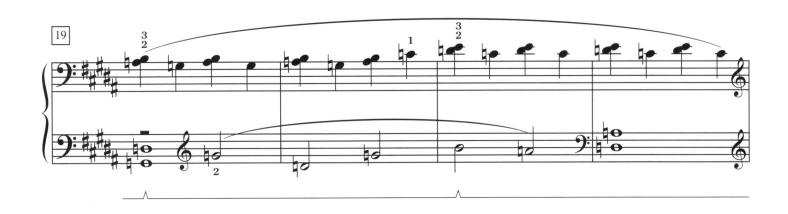

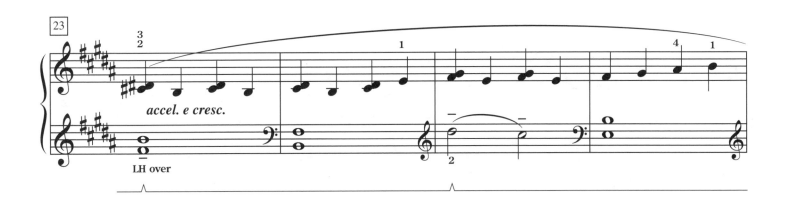

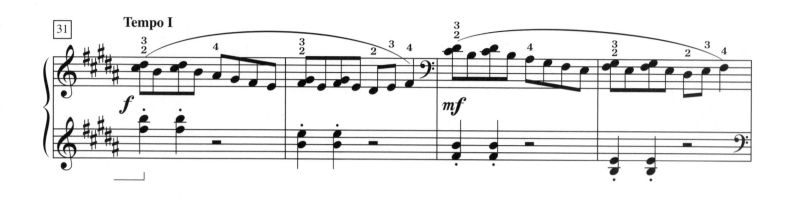

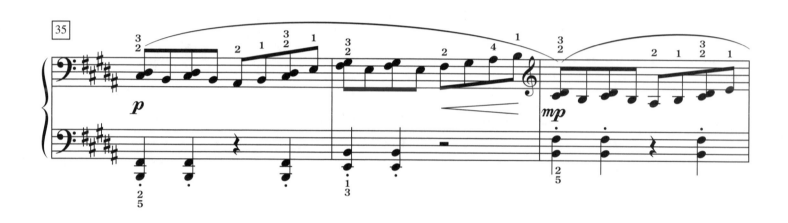

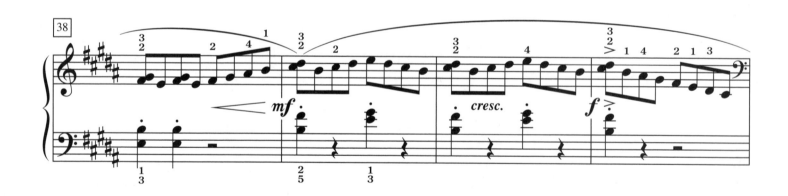

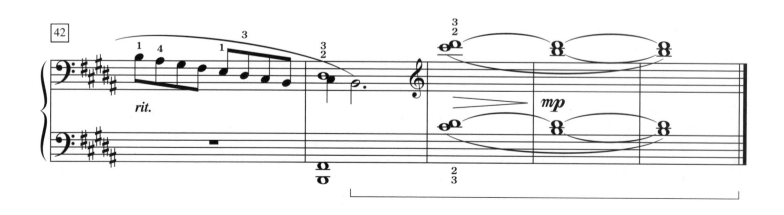

Prelude No. 22 in E♭ Minor

Robert D. Vandall

Moderate tempo, with gentle simplicity

Prelude No. 23 in F♯ Minor

Robert D. Vandall

Prelude No. 24 in B♭ Minor

Robert D. Vandall

Prelude No. 15 in C Minor

Robert D. Vandall

Prelude No. 16 in D♭ Major

Robert D. Vandall

*Be sure to lift hands and pedal before starting the next phrase.

44

Prelude No. 17 in E Major

Robert D. Vandall

Prelude No. 18 in F♯ Major

Robert D. Vandall

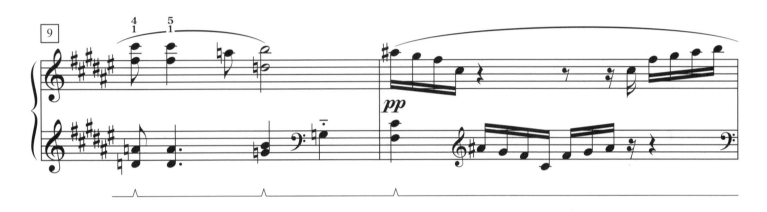

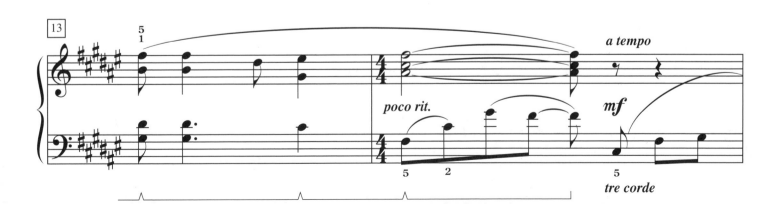

Prelude No. 19 in G♯ Minor

Robert D. Vandall

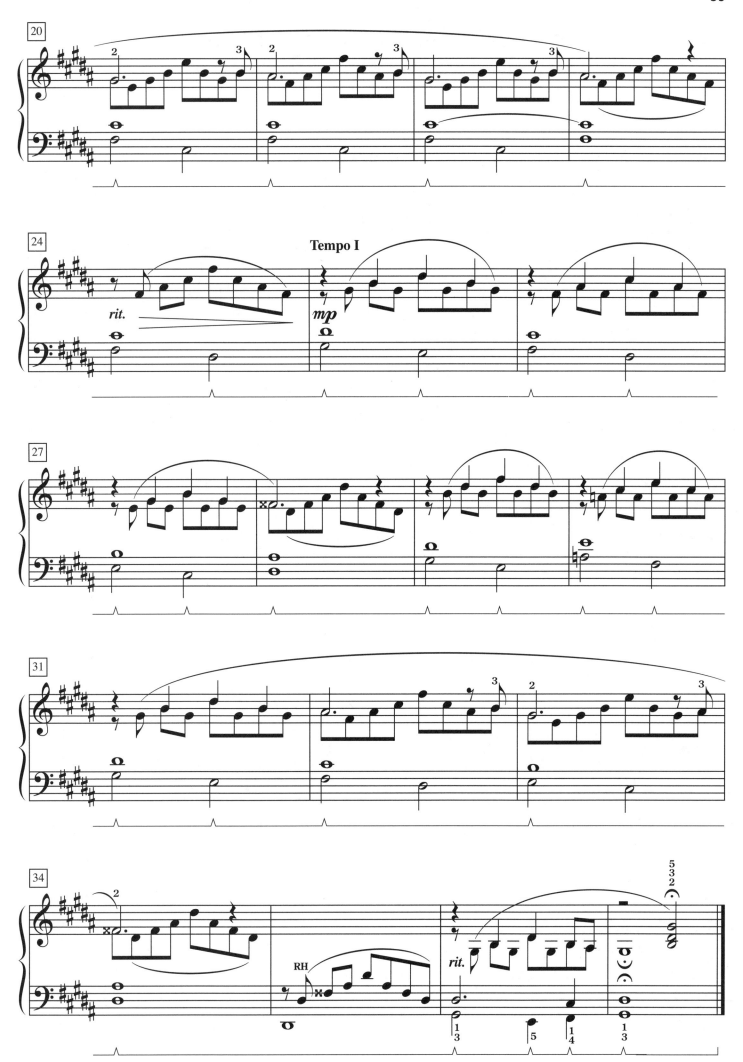

Prelude No. 20 in A Minor

Robert D. Vandall

Prelude No. 21 in B♭ Major

Robert D. Vandall

Merrily, but not too fast

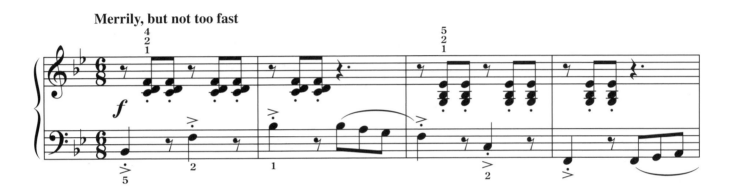